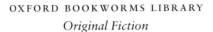

OXFORD BOOKWORMS LIBRARY
Original Fiction

The Silver Statue

PAUL SHIPTON

Starter (250 headwords)

T0345471

Illustrated by Berat Pekmezci/The Bright Agency

Series Editor: Rachel Bladon
Founder Editors: Jennifer Bassett
and Tricia Hedge

OXFORD
UNIVERSITY PRESS

Great Clarendon Street, Oxford, OX2 6DP, United Kingdom

Oxford University Press is a department of the University of Oxford.
It furthers the University's objective of excellence in research, scholarship,
and education by publishing worldwide. Oxford is a registered trade
mark of Oxford University Press in the UK and in certain other countries

ISBN: 978 0 19 463408 3

A complete recording of this Bookworms edition of *The Silver Statue* is available.

Printed in China

Word count (main text): 1,410

For more information on the Oxford Bookworms Library,
visit www.oup.com/elt/gradedreaders

ACKNOWLEDGEMENTS

Cover Image: Berat Pekmezci/The Bright Agency

Illustrations by: Berat Pekmezci/The Bright Agency

The publisher would like to thank the following for the permission to reproduce photographs:
123RF p.31 (street dancer/Michael spring); Oxford University Press pp.30 (cinema audience/
LuckyImages), 30 (women food shopping/Monkey Business Images), 30 (family enjoying meal/
Gareth Boden); Shutterstock pp.30 (shopping centre/S-F), 31 (circus juggler/Akos Horvath Stock
Photos), 31 (artist painting/Ventura), 31 (jazz street players/LightField Studios), 42 (Croatian
circus/Maljalen), 42 (friends playing guitar/De-V)

CONTENTS

CHAPTER 1
Guitar and Drums

My friend Kate *loves* music. She's always singing and playing her guitar, and she's good, too.

She usually plays in her bedroom, but today, she's going to play in the town square. She's going to play in front of people, and she's afraid. So I'm going with her. My name's Lucy and I'm Kate's best friend.

We arrive at the square and there are lots of people. Near the flower shop, there is a living statue. She is silver from head to foot. Her face, her hat, her coat… *everything*.

'She isn't moving!' I say. 'How does she *do* that?'

The man from the flower shop hears me. 'Oh, the silver statue never moves!' he laughs. 'She stands there every day, from early morning to late afternoon.'

We walk across the square and stop near a café. 'I'm going to sing here, I think,' says Kate. She gets her guitar out of its bag.

'Good luck,' I say.

'Thanks.'

Kate begins to sing and play her guitar. She's good, but she's usually better. She's afraid, I can see. Perhaps she's thinking, 'Are people going to like my music?'

But some people stop and listen, and soon, Kate is happier. She begins to play better.

Then, suddenly, everything changes. I hear something new – drums! LOUD drums!

A young man is sitting in the square and he's playing drums on three white buckets.

Kate sings louder, but it doesn't help. Nobody is listening now because nobody can hear her over the drums.

Kate stops playing. 'How can I play over that terrible noise?' she asks angrily.

(It isn't terrible; he's a good drummer, but I can't say *that* now!)

Kate puts her guitar in its bag.

'Let's have a drink at the café and wait,' I say.

At the café, Kate says, 'Those drums are *loud*!'

The woman from the café smiles. 'Oh, that's Joe,' she says. 'He plays here every Saturday.'

We finish our drinks and wait, but the drums don't stop.

'Let's go,' Kate says. 'We can come back next week.'

The silver statue watches us. Of course, she says nothing...

CHAPTER 2
An Early Morning

The next week, Kate wants to get an earlier bus.

'I don't know, Kate. I don't like getting up early on a Saturday,' I tell her.

'But I want to arrive at the square before that drummer. And I need you there. Please, Lucy.'

'OK,' I say.

Of course, the silver statue is there when we arrive.

Then we look across the square. Someone is sitting near the café. It's Joe with his drums!

'Look,' says Kate. '*He's* here early, too!' She begins walking fast across the square.

'Wait, Kate!' I say, but she doesn't listen to me.

'You're playing the drums here *again*,' Kate says.

Joe looks up and says, 'I always play here on a Saturday.'

'But you're very loud,' says Kate angrily.

I want to help. 'Perhaps you can play first,' I say to Joe, 'and then—'

But now, Joe is angry, too.

'This isn't *your* square!' he tells Kate, and then he begins playing.

'And *that* isn't music!' Kate shouts over the drums.

But Joe closes his eyes and plays.

'Let's go to the café again,' I say. 'We can wait there.'
But Kate is walking away. '*Next* week is going to be different…' she says.

CHAPTER 3
Louder and Louder

The next Saturday, we're back in the square.

The silver statue is there – of course – but we don't see Joe today.

Kate has her guitar, but that isn't all. She has an amp and a microphone, too. They're from our school.

When Kate begins playing this time, the music is louder. People stop and listen. They like her, I know it. Some people give her money. They put it in her guitar bag.

But when Kate is singing her third song, we suddenly hear drums. We look across the square and see Joe.

This time, Kate is ready. She doesn't stop playing – no, she smiles and turns up the amp. That's better!

But then Joe begins playing louder, too.

Kate turns up the amp again. Now her music is *very* loud.

But wait – the drums are louder now, too!

Some of the people in the square begin walking away. People can't hear Kate's music very well because Joe's drums are very loud. And they can't hear the drums well because Kate's song is loud, too. Together, they're making a terrible noise!

Suddenly, there is a shout: 'STOP!'

CHAPTER 4
A Note

'STOP!' someone shouts again. It's the woman from the café. Kate and Joe stop playing and look back at her.

'Nobody wants to hear this,' the woman says. She's right – *nobody* is sitting at the tables in front of her café now.

Kate and Joe walk across to the woman.

'Sorry,' they say.

'OK,' says the woman. 'Joe, you can play first, for thirty minutes.' She looks at Kate. 'Then *you* can play. All right?'

'Yes,' they say.

Kate and I sit at the café for the next thirty minutes. Of course, we can hear the drums.

But I can see something, too – under the table, Kate's foot is moving. She *likes* Joe's drums!

Soon, Joe finishes, and Kate begins playing. She sings well, and Joe listens to her.

After the last song, Kate and I take the money from her guitar bag.

'Wait,' I say. 'What's this? It's a note for you.'

'What does it say?' asks Kate.

Sorry about today. Your music is good! Perhaps we can play TOGETHER next week? 11 a.m. ?

I look up. 'It's from Joe, I think.'

On the bus home, I have only one question.

'So… are you going to meet Joe next week?'

'Perhaps,' Kate says. 'He *is* an OK drummer…'

I want to shout, 'And he has nice eyes!' But for Kate, music is everything!

CHAPTER 5
Silver Paint

The next Saturday, I arrive at the square after Kate. I find her with Joe near the café. They're talking before they play together.

Kate sees me and says, 'You're here! Thanks, Lucy.'

'That's OK,' I say. 'I want to hear this!'

Kate begins playing and singing, then Joe begins drumming. Kate plays this song a lot, but it's different with the drums – I like it!

Suddenly, I see something: Joe's bag is open and there's a note in it. The note says:

> *Sorry about today. Your music is good!*
> *Perhaps we can play TOGETHER next*
> *week? 11 a.m. ?*

This note and Kate's note are the same. And Joe's note is not from Kate! So, who are the notes from?

Then I see some paint on the note. *Silver* paint.

Just then, I hear something from across the square – some people are laughing. They're watching the silver statue.

First, her foot moves, then one leg... two legs... her arms... then her body.

'Look!' someone shouts. 'She's moving!'

I look at the silver statue. And now, she is DANCING. She's dancing to Kate and Joe's music!

Soon, lots of people are laughing and dancing, too. Kate and Joe's music is very good, and everyone is having a good time.

When the song finishes, the people all shout for more. Kate and Joe smile and begin a new song.

This time, the silver statue doesn't move – she's a statue again.

CHAPTER 6
The Secret

Kate and Joe play two more songs. When they stop, everyone wants to talk to them.

'Come back next week!' one woman says. 'I want the silver statue to dance again!'

'And I want to hear that music again,' says her friend.

The woman from the café is much happier now. 'You two are great!' she tells Kate and Joe. 'Are you going to play together again?'

'I'd like that,' says Kate.

'Me too,' Joe says. He smiles at Kate. 'And I'm sorry about last week.'

'I'm sorry, too,' says Kate. 'Do you want to talk about new songs one day this week? I can give you my number.'

'Yes, let's do that,' Joe says. 'And perhaps we can meet at the café one evening?'

Kate smiles back at him. 'Yes... I'd like that.'

She sees my face. 'What?' she says. 'Music isn't *everything*, you know, Lucy!'

Kate and Joe begin talking excitedly again. When they play music together, it's very good. And they're going to be good friends, I think.

We walk in front of the silver statue, and I think about the notes. I look up at her and see a little smile on her face.

I'm not going to tell Kate and Joe about the notes. That's *our* secret – me and the silver statue.

amp *(n)* An amp can make music louder.

bucket *(n)* a thing for carrying something, e.g. water

bus *(n)* a vehicle like a big, long car; it takes a lot of people along the road and stops often, and then people get on and off

café *(n)* You can get drinks and food in a café.

dance *(v)* to move your body with music

drum *(n)* a round thing; when you hit it, you make music; **drummer** *(n)* This person plays the drums.

guitar *(n)* You make music when you play the guitar (a thing with six long strings) with your hand.

living statue *(n)* a person for people to look at; they dress in an interesting way and do not move

loud *(adj)* making a lot of noise

microphone *(n)* With a microphone, you can sing or speak louder.

music *(n)* the sounds when you sing, or play musical instruments, e.g. a guitar or drums

note *(n)* a small letter; some writing

paint *(n)* With paint, you can change the colour of something or make a picture.

same *(adj)* not different

secret *(n)* When you don't want people to know something.

shout *(v)* to speak very loudly

silver *(adj)* this colour: ●

song *(n)* music with words

square *(n)* an open place in a town with buildings in front and behind; often it is nice to sit in a square

terrible *(adj)* very bad

together *(adv)* with someone

turn up *(v)* to make something louder

In a Town

shopping centre

cinema

supermarket

restaurant

Do you often go into town? When? Who with?

Where do you like to go in town?

Street Performers

juggler

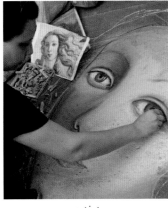

artist

dancer

musician

Which of these performers would you like to see or listen to?

Which performer would you most like to be?

The Silver Statue

ACTIVITIES

Think Ahead

1 Look at the back cover and title. Are these things true?
Write ✓ (yes) or ✗ (no).

   1 Kate doesn't like playing the guitar. ☐

   2 Kate and Joe play music in the town square
one Saturday. ☐

   3 Kate and Lucy are friends. ☐

   4 Joe plays the drums. ☐

2 Look at the story title, cover, and contents page. What do
you think is going to happen in these chapters?

   1 Chapter 2: An Early Morning:
Who gets up early?

   2 Chapter 4: A Note:
Who writes a note?

   3 Chapter 5: Silver Paint:
Where is the silver paint?

3 **RESEARCH** Before you read, find pictures of living statues.
Do you like them? Why/Why not?

Chapter Check

CHAPTER 1 Choose the correct words.

1 Kate loves to *play / listen to* the guitar.

2 Lucy and Kate are *best friends / sisters*.

3 The silver statue in the square never *leaves / moves*.

4 Kate sings near a *flower shop / café*.

5 Kate can't play music because the *people in the square / drums* are loud.

6 Kate and Lucy *work / wait* in the café.

CHAPTER 2 Are the sentences true or false?

1 The next week, Lucy wants to get up early.

2 The silver statue arrives at the square before Kate and Lucy.

3 When Kate and Lucy arrive, Joe is there with his drums.

4 Joe comes to the square every Saturday.

5 Kate and Lucy wait in the café again.

CHAPTER 3 Put sentences a–f in the correct order.

a Joe begins drumming.

b Kate and Lucy go to the square.

c Kate begins singing and playing with a microphone and an amp.

d Kate turns up the amp and plays louder.

e Someone shouts, 'Stop!'

f People begin walking away because the music is loud.

CHAPTER 4 Match the sentence halves.

1 Kate and Joe stop…

2 Joe plays first and…

3 Kate moves her foot…

4 Kate begins playing and…

5 Lucy finds a note…

6 On the bus, Lucy and Kate…

a in Kate's guitar bag.

b Joe listens.

c talk about Joe.

d playing.

e under the table.

f Kate waits in the café.

CHAPTER 5 Choose a, b, or c.

1 Who does Lucy find when she arrives at the square?
   a the woman from the café   b Joe and Kate
   c the silver statue

2 What does Lucy see in Joe's bag?
   a a note   b flowers   c a guitar

3 What is the silver statue doing?
   a singing   b dancing   c playing the drums

4 Kate and Joe's music is…
   a loud.   b terrible.   c good.

CHAPTER 6 Complete the sentences with the correct words.

is   meet   play   says   talk   tell

1 When Kate and Joe stop playing, people in the square
   want to _____ to them.

2 The woman from the café _____ happy now.

3 Kate and Joe want to _____ together again.

4 Joe _____ sorry to Kate.

5 They are going to _____ at the café in the week.

6 Lucy isn't going to _____ Kate and Joe about the
   notes from the silver statue.

Focus on Vocabulary

1 Match the words to the sentences.

café   note   paint   same   secret   terrible

1 'Please don't tell people about this!'
2 'Let's go for a hot drink there.'
3 'I'm going to change the colour of my room.'
4 'Heidi has long, dark hair. Ann has long, dark hair, too!'
5 'I'm quickly writing this for my dad because I don't want him to forget about this evening.'
6 'Oh no! That's very, very bad!'

2 Replace the <u>underlined</u> words with the words below.

amp   bucket   bus   guitar   silver   square

1 The paint is <u>loud</u>.
2 A <u>microphone</u> is a place in a town or city.
3 Turn up the <u>drummer</u> for louder music.
4 You can carry water in a <u>note</u>.
5 A <u>living statue</u> is a musical instrument.
6 A <u>café</u> carries people into town.

Focus on Language

1 Complete the sentences with the correct form of
   be going to for future.

   1 Today, Kate _____ play the guitar in front
      of people.

   2 I _____ go with her to the square.

   3 The people _____ like her music.

   4 Kate _____ sing near the café.

   5 Kate and Joe _____ play together again.

   6 Kate _____ meet Joe next week.

2 **DECODE** Read this text from the story. Look at the
   pronouns 1–5. Who do they describe?

The next Saturday, I arrive at the square after Kate. I find
¹her with Joe near the café. ²They're talking before they
play together.
   Kate sees ³me and says, '⁴You're here! Thanks, Lucy.'
'That's OK,' I say. '⁵I want to hear this!'

   1 a Kate   b Lucy

   2 a Kate and Joe   b Kate and Lucy

   3 a Kate   b Lucy

   4 a Lucy   b Kate

   5 a Joe   b Lucy

Discussion

1 Read. Complete the dialogue with *because* or *so*.

LUCAS: The silver statue writes a note to Kate, and she writes the same note to Joe. I think that's <u>terrible</u> ¹_____ Kate and Joe don't know. What do you think?

JULIA: I don't agree. The silver statue wants to help, ²_____ she writes those notes. It's <u>nice</u>! Do you agree, Simon?

SIMON: Yes, I agree. For me, it's <u>OK</u> when she writes the notes. But what about Lucy? Kate is happy, ³_____ Lucy doesn't tell her about the notes. But is that OK?

LUCAS: No! I think that's <u>bad</u>, too! Secrets are always bad!

JULIA: For me, it is <u>not very bad</u>. Lucy doesn't tell Kate and Joe ⁴_____ they're friends now and they are happy.

2 Read the dialogue again and complete the phrases.

1 What do you _____?

2 I _____ agree. / I agree.

3 Do you _____?

4 But what _____ … ?

5 I _____ that…

6 For _____, …

3 **Which of the phrases in exercise 2 are used for:**

a giving your opinion?

b asking for somebody's opinion?

c agreeing or disagreeing with somebody's opinion?

4 **Look at the dialogue in exercise 1 again. Put the underlined words in the right place on the line below.**

negative (−)   positive (+)

5 **THINK CRITICALLY** **Discuss the sentences about the story with a partner. Use** *because*, **the phrases from exercise 2, and the words from exercise 4.**

1 Joe begins playing the drums before Kate begins playing. (page 9)

2 Kate turns up her amp. (page 13)

3 The woman from the café shouts at Kate and Joe. (page 15)

1 Read the poster about the Street Performer Day. Would you like to go? Why/Why not?

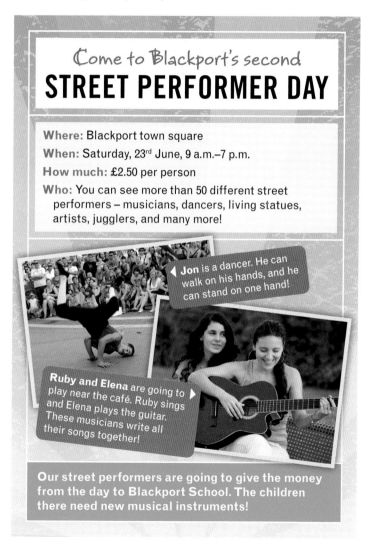

Come to Blackport's second

STREET PERFORMER DAY

Where: Blackport town square

When: Saturday, 23rd June, 9 a.m.–7 p.m.

How much: £2.50 per person

Who: You can see more than 50 different street performers – musicians, dancers, living statues, artists, jugglers, and many more!

◄ **Jon** is a dancer. He can walk on his hands, and he can stand on one hand!

Ruby and Elena are going to play near the café. Ruby sings and Elena plays the guitar. These musicians write all their songs together! ►

Our street performers are going to give the money from the day to Blackport School. The children there need new musical instruments!

2 **Answer the questions about the Street Performer Day.**

1 Where is the Street Performer Day going to be?

2 What time is it going to begin and finish?

3 How many street performers are going to be there?

4 What can Jon stand on?

5 Who writes the songs for Ruby and Elena?

6 Why does the school need money?

3 COMMUNICATE **Ask other students the questions.**

1 Can you sing?

2 Can you play a musical instrument? (Which one?)

3 Can you dance well?

4 Are you a good artist / juggler / living statue?

4 COLLABORATE **Work in a group. Plan a Street Performer Day for your town. Discuss the questions.**

1 Where and when is the day going to be?

2 Who are the performers going to be?

3 Who is going to come and watch the performers?

4 Are you going to ask for any money? (What are you going to do with it?)

5 CREATE **Make a poster about your Street Performer Day.**

If you liked this Bookworm, why not try...

Sing to Win

STARTER
Andrea Sarto

Sing to Win is the biggest programme on TV – everyone watches it and every singer wants to win it. Sofia loves singing, so she goes to an audition for *Sing to Win* – and makes friends with Emma. Emma is a very good singer, too, and soon there are stories about the two friends on TV and online. But not all the stories are true – and suddenly, being friends is not easy...

The Big Game

STARTER
Paul Shipton

West High School boys' basketball team is the worst team in town – everyone knows that. They always lose. But that's OK – Ben and his friends love playing. Then they get a new player. Sam is good, very good. Suddenly everything changes for the West High team, and Ben is excited. But is winning games the most important thing?
